Kiss and Make Up

T. P. Turner

Fearon
Belmont, California

DOUBLE FASTBACK® ROMANCE Books

Cover illustrator: Terry Hoff

Copyright © 1987 by David S. Lake Publishers,
19 Davis Drive, Belmont, California 94002. All rights
reserved. No part of this book may be reproduced
by any means, transmitted, or translated into a
machine language without written permission from
the publisher.
ISBN 0-8224-2384-7
Library of Congress Catalog Card Number: 86-81653
Printed in the United States of America
1. 9 8 7 6 5 4 3 2 1

Abbie Chang locked her bike to the fence next to Dr. Stein's office. Before going inside, she stepped back to admire the brand-new ten-speed. It was her pride and joy. Then she wedged her helmet under her arm and walked over to unlock the office door.

Abbie was the receptionist in Dr. Stein's dental office. As usual, she was the first to arrive. She hung up her yellow windbreaker and her helmet in the closet and took a quick look in the mirror. All she had to do was to run her fingers through her shiny, short black hair to make it look just right. Then she whisked a touch of blusher over her pale cheeks and flicked some mascara onto her long lashes. That was all the makeup she ever wore.

As Abbie organized her desk to get ready for the day's appointments, she hummed one of her favorite songs. Also, she thought about Ben.

Ben Wong was the assistant to Dr. Howell, the vet who took care of Abbie's cat, Oliver. Abbie had met Ben in Dr.

Howell's office. And she had liked him immediately. First, his dark good looks had attracted her. But then Abbie had noticed how gentle Ben was with her cat. Oliver hadn't even put up a fight when Dr. Howell gave him his shots. And finally, there was the wonderful smile Ben had given her when he'd said, "I hope I don't have to wait for Oliver's next checkup to see you again." Once home, Abbie had hugged Oliver to thank him for introducing her to Ben.

They had been dating for a little over a month now, since the beginning of June. During that time, Abbie hadn't even wanted to go out with another guy. She still thought Ben was just as nice as he had seemed that first day in Dr. Howell's office. And Abbie was delighted to find that he loved biking, too. They had already taken several long bike trips together. Each time, they had taken a picnic lunch and had thoroughly enjoyed each other's company.

Abbie was sure that Ben wasn't dating anyone else, either. He spent so much time with Abbie that he couldn't possibly find time for other dates. Also, Ben didn't seem like the kind of guy who would date a lot of women. But nothing had actually been said on the subject. Abbie hoped that Ben would soon say something about wanting to be her steady boyfriend.

Abbie's thoughts were interrupted by the telephone.

"Good morning. Dr. Stein's office," Abbie said in her cheerful, professional-sounding voice. The sound of a barking dog on the other end of the line told her it was Ben.

"Good morning," Ben said. "I'd like to speak to Dr. Stein's cute receptionist."

"Wait one moment, please," Abbie laughed. "I'll see if she's in." Then she said, "Hi! What's up?"

"You know Jill, the receptionist here?" Ben asked. "Well, she just quit. A cocker spaniel puppy had a little accident on her foot, and she got hysterical. You should've seen her. She said she was sick of being around disgusting animals all day. She's going to find a job working with humans."

"She may be sorry," commented Abbie, thinking grimly of the way some of Dr. Stein's patients acted.

"That's exactly what I told her," said Ben. "But the thing is, Dr. Howell needs a new receptionist right away. I was thinking you could apply for the job."

"Oh, I don't know," said Abbie. She was pleased that Ben wanted her to work with him, but her loyalty to Dr. Stein made her reluctant to leave. She had also heard that mixing work with romance could only lead to problems.

"Come on," urged Ben. "You'd be perfect for the job. You love animals, and you're really good with them. Plus, it would be great to work together. We'd have so much fun."

"It does sound like fun," Abbie agreed, "but I'd feel terrible leaving Dr. Stein. He hired me with no experience and taught me everything I know about running an office. And he's always been really nice to me. It wouldn't seem right to just quit."

"I see what you mean," Ben admitted. "Oh well, it was a nice thought."

Just then, Abbie heard footsteps coming up the stairs outside. She didn't want Dr. Stein to find her spending time on a personal call first thing in the morning.

"I've got to go. Good-bye," she said to Ben.

Dr. Stein walked into the office looking very serious. "Good morning, Abbie," he said. "I'd like to see you in my office, please."

Abbie wondered what was wrong. Quickly, she followed Dr. Stein into his office.

"Sit down, Abbie," he said, motioning to an armchair next to his large, cluttered desk. He took a seat behind the desk. "I need to tell you that I've made an important decision. I'm afraid it could make things difficult for you. You see, I'm getting older, and I've never had enough time to spend with my wife and grandchildren. So I've decided to retire in September. I wanted to tell you right away, to give you plenty of time to find a new job. Of course, I will give you the highest recommendation."

"Actually, Dr. Stein, I have a lead on a job already," Abbie replied. "I wasn't going to follow it up, but now I guess I will."

The warnings Abbie had heard about mixing work with romance were instantly forgotten. She thought of her cozy apartment—the first one of her very own—and her new bike, for which she was still paying. She couldn't afford to be out of work. And, in spite of the warnings, the idea of working in the same office as Ben was very tempting.

Abbie dialed Dr. Howell's office to tell Ben of the new development.

"Great!" Ben exclaimed. "I'll tell Dr. Howell you'll be here at noon."

At 11:45, Abbie was on her way out the door. In her purse was a letter of recommendation from Dr. Stein. It was so full of praise that it could have gotten her a job as president of the United States. Abbie felt a little embarrassed when she read it, but Dr. Stein had said, "Everything in that letter is absolutely true."

Abbie unlocked her bike and pedaled the short distance to the vet's office. Once there, she locked up her bike, took off her helmet, and straightened her hair a bit. Walking through the doorway, she took a deep breath to calm her slightly shaky nerves.

"Of course I remember you," Dr. Howell said, smiling as Ben introduced Abbie. "You're Oliver's owner. Come have a seat in my office."

The interview went well. Abbie could tell by the expression on Dr. Howell's face that he was impressed by the letter from Dr. Stein.

"Well, Abbie," said Dr. Howell, looking up from his desk, "you seem to meet all the requirements."

Abbie just replied, "I always try to do my best."

"This place is a bit more hectic than a dentist's office because animals are less predictable than people," Dr. Howell pointed out. "Ben told you what happened to my last receptionist."

"Yes," Abbie said, laughing. "But I've handled some difficult people. I'm sure I can manage."

"So am I," said Dr. Howell, "which is why I'm hiring you. There's just one more thing I want to mention before we shake hands and call it a deal."

"What's that?" asked Abbie.

"I know this is a delicate subject, but it's better to bring it up now than later," Dr. Howell began, looking serious. "You and Ben have been dating. I want the two of you to make sure that whatever goes on between you does not interfere with your jobs. I'm trusting you both to be sensible enough to keep your personal lives separate from your jobs."

Abbie knew that Dr. Howell was right. "I've thought about that," she admitted. "I'm sure that Ben and I can handle the situation wisely."

Dr. Howell stood up and extended his hand. "Then welcome to our staff, Abbie," he said, smiling as he grasped her hand in a friendly handshake.

Abbie didn't have to say a word to Ben when she came out of Dr. Howell's office. It was obvious from her expression that she had gotten the job.

"When do you start?" he asked.

"Two weeks from Monday," she answered. "I can't wait."

"Then let's celebrate tonight," Ben suggested.

Abbie rode her bike home and, after saying hello to Oliver, changed into her teal blue dress. She rarely wore skirts or dresses, but tonight was special.

"You look beautiful," said Ben when she opened the door. Abbie knew Ben thought she was pretty. Tonight, though, his look made her feel truly beautiful.

"You look great, too," she said, returning the compliment. Ben was wearing jeans, but he had on a light blue shirt and a white linen sports jacket. Abbie felt elegant as they walked into Richard's, an excellent restaurant just a few blocks from her apartment. The tables were set with pink tablecloths and napkins and beautiful china. On each table was a candle and a small vase of fresh daisies. The candlelight gave the room a warm glow.

The dinner of seafood and steak was wonderful. Afterward, sipping coffee out of delicate china cups, Ben and Abbie held hands across the table.

"I have something I'd like to say," Ben began.

Abbie held her breath. Could this be what she had been hoping for?

"What is it, Ben?" she whispered.

"I've been wanting to say this for a while," Ben continued, "but I was always afraid it was too soon. I've never had so much fun with anyone. And I've never felt so—well— so right about anyone else. I'm in love with you, Abbie."

"I love you, too, Ben," Abbie answered, her voice quavering.

"I don't want to date anyone but you," Ben continued. "I hope you feel the same way?" His voice rose in a question.

"Of course I do," Abbie responded immediately. "I haven't even looked at another guy since we started dating. Oh, Ben, I've never been so happy. This is just what I've been hoping for!" Ben smiled his approval, and the two sat staring into each other's eyes for several moments.

When they left the restaurant, they sat on a bench beside a pond just outside. Abbie felt completely content. She turned her face toward Ben for a long, wonderful kiss. Then Abbie rested her head on his shoulder. She could feel his hand stroking her hair.

Later, they walked hand in hand toward Abbie's apartment. It was then that Abbie told Ben what Dr. Howell had said about not letting their personal lives interfere with work.

"No problem," said Ben. "We'll be smart about it. Everything'll work out great. In fact, right now, I'd say life is just about perfect."

Abbie had to agree.

A little more than two weeks later, Abbie rode her bike to Dr. Howell's office. She parked her bike next to Ben's. As soon as she entered the office, she noticed the beautiful vase of flowers sitting on her desk. She didn't need to ask where they had come from.

"Thank you," Abbie said, beaming at Ben as he appeared from around the corner. She gave him a quick hug and kiss before sitting down at her desk. She wanted to look efficient when Dr. Howell came in.

"OK, we're at work now," said Ben. "So let's get down to business." His voice sounded almost stern, but his eyes betrayed how happy he was to have Abbie there. He went over the office routine and book-keeping procedures with her. Abbie was surprised at how similar a vet's office was to a dentist's.

"This is going to be a breeze," she said.

"Wait till the animals start coming in," Ben warned.

Half an hour later, the office had become crowded with people and their animals. The air was filled with barking, meowing, and arguing. Ben was in the examining room helping Dr. Howell with a dog who had a broken leg.

In a corner of the waiting room, a poodle small enough to fit into its owner's purse was yapping continuously. In another corner sat a man with a Siamese cat. A few seats away from him was a woman with a solemn-looking German shepherd at her feet.

"That beast should be on a leash," said the man to the woman with the shepherd. The cat was hissing and spitting at the dog, who looked worried.

"Why don't you sit on the other side of the room?" asked the woman. "Melissa is the only animal here who is behaving herself."

"Why don't *you* move?" asked the man with the cat. "We were here first. And speaking of behaving, that dog looks like the one who's been knocking over my garbage can every morning. Maybe if you'd keep it tied up, it'd behave."

The German shepherd barked once in self-defense, as if she understood the accusation. That sent the cat flying to the far corner of the waiting room, where he stood with his back arched and his tail raised. A chain reaction started. The poodle jumped out of his owner's purse and ran toward the door, which opened to admit a woman carrying a rabbit in a cardboard box. The poodle, still yapping, began nipping at the woman's ankles and jumping up around her legs.

"Help!" the woman screamed. "This dog is attacking Princess!"

"Pierre," coaxed the poodle's owner, "come back to Mommy now. Leave nice Princess alone." But Pierre went right on yapping, nipping, and jumping.

Abbie had to do something. She came out from behind her desk, picked up Pierre, and returned him to his owner. "Please hold him on your lap, ma'am," she asked the woman politely.

"Don't you yell at me, young lady!" cried the poodle's owner indignantly. "It was the cat's fault."

Abbie was about to reply when Ben entered the waiting room. Within seconds, he had calmed both animals and owners.

"How did you manage that?" whispered Abbie, impressed.

"It's easy, when you get to know everyone," Ben reassured her. "You'll be able to do it soon. You're doing fine already. Who's next?"

"Mrs. Hanson, you can take Melissa in now," Abbie said to the German shepherd's owner.

"I was here first," objected the owner of the Siamese cat, "and Gabriel is getting nervous."

"Yes, I know," answered Abbie firmly, "but Mrs. Hanson's appointment was earlier."

Gabriel was still hissing, but Abbie knew how to comfort cats. She stroked him calmly, and then rubbed his ears and scratched him under the chin. Before long, he was purring. His owner settled down with a magazine.

Abbie heard the telephone ring and returned to her desk to answer it.

"Good morning. Dr. Howell's office," she said.

"Hello," said a female voice. "Is Ben there?"

Abbie was surprised. "He's with a patient right now. Perhaps I can help you," she offered.

"No, thanks," the woman said. "I don't have any pets. I'm just a friend of Ben's. Will you tell him Suzanne called?"

"Certainly," said Abbie, trying to sound calm and professional. "Would you care to leave your number so he can reach you?"

"Oh, that's OK," Suzanne said. "He knows my number. Thanks a lot." Then she hung up.

Abbie was puzzled and hurt. "Who is Suzanne?" she wondered. Ben had never mentioned her. And he had just told Abbie he loved *her* and didn't want to date anyone else. So why was this woman calling him? By now, Abbie was so upset her hands were shaking. She could feel tears welling up in her eyes. But she remembered what Dr. Howell had said about keeping her personal life separate from work. "I need this job," she thought. "I'm not going to let a stupid phone call ruin it for me." She forced herself to concentrate on her work.

When Ben came out with Melissa, Abbie smiled sweetly at the Siamese cat's owner and said, "Gabriel can go in now."

Ben walked past her, carrying the cat. "Suzanne called," Abbie said, without looking at him. "She wants you to call her back."

"Thanks," was all Ben said.

"She said you already know her number," Abbie added, pronouncing each word coldly and distinctly. But her angry tone seemed lost on Ben, who disappeared into the examining room with Gabriel.

Abbie hardly talked to Ben for the rest of the day. She was still angry, but she didn't want to argue with Ben at work. After they closed the office that evening, Ben and Abbie walked to the parking lot in silence.

"What's bothering you?" Ben asked, unlocking his bike.

Abbie looked at him angrily. Now all the frustration and rage that had built up during the day started to come out.

"Who is Suzanne," she demanded, "and why is she calling you?"

As soon as she spoke, she saw Ben's expression harden. He stared at her coldly through eyes that looked almost cruel. Abbie took a step backward.

"Now, wait a minute," Ben said in a voice that matched his expression. "You can ask me anything you want, but not in that tone of voice. I don't like being questioned like some kind of criminal."

Abbie felt her anger grow. Wasn't he the one who was getting phone calls from other women? What right did *he* have to be angry?

"Well, who is she?" Abbie repeated, deliberately using the tone that Ben so obviously disliked.

"She's a friend of mine," Ben answered coldly.

"A friend?" Abbie asked in amazement. "After we just promised not to date anyone else, that's all the explanation you have?"

"Listen, Abbie, I'm *not* dating anyone else. I meant everything I said to you Friday night. But I never said I wanted you running my life. And I won't have you telling me who my friends can be."

Abbie couldn't believe she and Ben were having a fight. Everything had seemed so perfect, and now it seemed just horrible.

"Well, I don't like her calling you," she said, fighting back tears. "How would you like it if I were friends with guys you've never even heard of?"

"Abbie, you can be friends with anyone you want, and so can I," Ben said defensively. "And if I have to lose you to keep my friends and my freedom, then that's the way it'll have to be." Ben got on his bike and rode away.

Abbie had a hard time sleeping that night. She wasn't sure who was right and who was wrong in this argument. Several times she had almost called Ben to apologize, but each time she decided against it. Even if she *had* been too quick to question Ben, he'd had no right to be so mean to her.

The next morning, Abbie wondered how she could possibly face going to work. She wished she could stay home, but it was only the second day of her new job. She got dressed, drank a cup of coffee, and rode to the office.

Although she felt terrible, Abbie somehow managed to get through the day. She and Ben spoke to each other only when necessary. The only time Ben acted friendly toward Abbie was when Dr. Howell was around.

Wednesday started out the same way Tuesday had. Abbie felt miserable. Just before noon the phone rang. She answered it and immediately recognized Suzanne's voice.

"Hello, is Ben there?" Suzanne asked sweetly.

"He's busy right now. May I ask who is calling?" Abbie said, although she knew perfectly well who it was.

"Yes, this is his friend Suzanne," came the reply. "Would you ask him to call me on his lunch break?"

"Yes, I will. I'm sure he has your number," said Abbie a bit sarcastically.

A few minutes later, she heard the examining room door open. "I wonder how he'd like a taste of his own medicine," Abbie said to herself. She quietly picked up the receiver, even though no one was on the line. "Thanks for calling, Jim," she said to the imaginary caller. "I'll see you at eight tonight." She paused for a moment to hand Ben a note that read: "Suzanne called. Please call her back."

"Good-bye, Jim," she said into the receiver and then hung up. "The phone's free now," she said casually to Ben as she walked out the door.

Abbie walked around town aimlessly during her lunch hour. She knew Ben had heard her made-up conversation, but she couldn't tell whether it had bothered him or not.

By Thursday, Abbie began to wonder how much longer she could pretend she didn't care. She still loved Ben, and she realized more and more that she had been at least partly to blame for their argument. And even if she weren't, proving her point wasn't worth the pain that their increasing unfriendliness was causing her. She decided to talk to Ben after work. She wanted to try to smooth things out.

Just as she made her decision, the telephone rang. It was Suzanne. "Does she call every day?" Abbie wondered. But to her surprise, Suzanne did not ask for Ben.

"Is this Abbie?" Suzanne asked.

"Yes, it is," Abbie answered.

"This is Suzanne. You know, Ben's friend," Suzanne explained. "Listen, if you have any free time on your lunch break today, I'd really like to talk to you. Would that be OK?"

Abbie hesitated. "How can I meet face-to-face with the person who's behind this whole mess?" she thought. Still, Suzanne did sound friendly and sincere. Maybe the argument with Ben really wasn't Suzanne's fault. Besides, she had to admit she was curious. What could Suzanne want to talk about?

"That would be fine," she said to Suzanne. "Where should I meet you?"

"How about the Sunflower, that sandwich shop up the street from your office?" Suzanne suggested. "Can you be there in ten minutes?"

"Sure. See you there," Abbie replied. She hung up the phone, grabbed her purse, and quickly left the office.

Ten minutes later, Abbie entered the sandwich shop and looked around uncertainly. A woman sitting alone in a booth waved to her. The woman was very pretty, with long blond hair and a great tan. "That must be Suzanne," thought Abbie.

"Thanks for coming, Abbie," the pretty blond began as Abbie slid into the booth. "I need to talk to you about Ben. First of all, Ben and I are just friends. In fact, I'm engaged to another man. I used to go out with Ben, but that was a long time ago. Ben is a sweetheart, but we didn't have enough in common. You know how he loves sports? Well, I'm not athletic at all. I'm even allergic to animals! Anyway, we still talk to each other a lot, even though we don't see each other much. Last night he asked if he could come over to talk. He was so miserable over this fight between you two. And he was going crazy with jealousy because he knew you had a date. He really wanted to call you, but he knew you'd be out. And I think his pride got in the way, too."

Abbie was too stunned to say anything. She let Suzanne go on.

"Ben's really in love with you, Abbie," Suzanne continued. "I'm sure you two can work things out if you just talk to him. But there's one thing you should know about Ben. He hates to have anyone order him around. I'm sure he would have introduced me to you soon, but he's got to do things in his own way and in his own time. If he feels like he's being pushed or threatened, look out!"

"I know what you mean," Abbie said slowly. "I had already made up my mind to talk to Ben tonight. But do you think he'd be mad if he knew we'd been talking like this?"

"I don't care if he is," Suzanne said with a shrug. "He'll get over it. I care too much about him to watch him suffer over a misunderstanding with someone he loves. And besides," she said with a little smile, "I never said I *wouldn't* call you. I have a feeling he wanted me to."

"Well, I'm certainly glad you did," Abbie said gratefully. "Thanks a lot. You've helped me understand Ben a little better.

And I may have even learned a little about myself."

The two women ordered sandwiches and talked some more as they ate. When they finished, Abbie thanked Suzanne again before hurrying back to the office.

That evening, Abbie purposely left the office at the same time that Ben did. He pretended not to notice her until they were outside.

"Hi," he said tonelessly as he started unlocking his bike.

"Could we talk for a minute?" Abbie asked, her voice shaking a bit.

"OK," Ben answered.

"I miss you a lot," said Abbie. She started to cry, even though she had been determined not to. Ben gently put his arms around her and said he missed her, too.

This made her cry even harder. When Abbie could speak again, she told Ben about her talk with Suzanne. She made sure he understood that she'd been planning to speak to him anyway.

"I really do understand why you got mad at me," she said.

"I understand how you felt, too," said Ben. He paused to give Abbie a kiss. "I should have told you about Suzanne right from the start."

"Thanks for saying that," Abbie said. "So everything's OK now?" she asked, wanting to make sure everything was settled.

"Except for one thing," said Ben. "What about your date last night?"

Abbie looked embarrassed. "I, uh . . . I faked that conversation to make you jealous," she admitted. "I'm really sorry. I spent most of my time last night thinking about what to say to you today."

Abbie and Ben kissed again and held each other for a long time.

"Why don't you come to my place for dinner?" Ben suggested. "I'll get the pizza; you bring the candles."

"I'll be there at seven," Abbie promised. She got on her bike and blew a kiss to Ben as she pedaled away.

Friday morning, Abbie was relieved to wake up without that empty feeling she'd felt all week. She had her usual breakfast of juice, cereal, and coffee while Oliver ate his tuna fish. When they had both finished, Abbie bent down and scratched Oliver behind the ears.

"Oliver, I think everything's going to be fine," she told the cat happily. Oliver didn't share her enthusiasm. He was too busy batting his toy mouse around the floor to pay attention. Abbie said good-bye to him and then biked to work.

As she neared the office, she saw Ben coming from the other direction. They parked their bikes, and Ben gave Abbie a quick kiss before they went into the office together.

Abbie looked at the appointment book. "Oh, no," she said to Ben. "Pierre is coming in again. He's such a little troublemaker."

"You'd be neurotic too if your mother carried you around in a purse," Ben replied, laughing.

"Mother?" asked Abbie, opening a letter.

"Well, she calls herself 'Mommy' when she talks to him," Ben pointed out.

"That's true," Abbie agreed. "And they do sort of look alike."

Ben and Abbie both laughed. It was true. Mrs. Velez did have a very poodlelike face.

Abbie thought about how much fun it was to work with Ben. Talking about the animals and their owners gave them more in common and made their relationship closer.

As the days went by, Abbie grew to like her job more and more. She also grew to be more efficient. Already, she had streamlined the bookkeeping system and reorganized the files. She had also created a newspaper-lined "puppy corner" in the waiting room. It was obvious that Dr. Howell was impressed with the way Abbie had taken charge of the office. Only one thing disturbed her. It seemed that the more confident she became, the less Ben kidded around with her. He kept more to himself in the office than he had when she had first started.

On Monday morning of Abbie's fourth week on the job, a man named Mr. Grant brought in a wiggly ginger-colored puppy. "Please wait here with Ginger for a few minutes while I get things ready for her blood test," Ben said to Mr. Grant. The man took a seat.

"Oh, Mr. Grant," said Abbie, "excuse me, but would you mind putting Ginger in the puppy corner?"

"Sure," said Mr. Grant, changing his seat.

Abbie turned to Ben. "Could you remember to keep the puppies in the puppy corner?" she asked.

Ben gave Abbie an angry look, but she was too busy typing up invoices to notice. Ben took Ginger into the examining room. In about 15 minutes, they were back.

"Ginger will be fine, Mr. Grant," Ben said. "She just needs to take the rest of her medicine. You can take her home now."

The waiting room was empty when Mr. Grant left. Ben walked behind Abbie's chair to return Ginger's folder to the filing cabinet.

"Ben," said Abbie without looking up, "please just leave the folder on my desk. I'd like to go over the new filing system with you again so things won't get confused."

"The filing system was fine the way it was," said Ben angrily.

Abbie looked up in surprise.

"In fact," Ben continued, "so was everything else before you came here."

Abbie couldn't believe what she was hearing. She stared at Ben in hurt silence as he kept talking.

"You've done nothing but try to take over since you got here," he said. "I didn't get you this job so you could push me around."

Abbie was terrified that Dr. Howell would hear them. But she couldn't control her rising anger. "Wait just a minute," she demanded. "You didn't get me this job. I got it myself. And I'm good at it, too. If you can't handle that, it's not my problem." Ben glared at her, and then turned and stomped out of the office.

Abbie and Ben didn't speak to each other for the rest of the day. After the last patient left, Abbie raced down the hall and out to her bike before Ben could leave the office.

She was out of breath when she entered her apartment. She picked up Oliver, buried her face in his soft gray fur, and sobbed.

"I hate him!" she told Oliver. "Even if he begs me to forgive him, I won't."

Abbie curled up on the sofa with Oliver and cried until she fell asleep. When the telephone rang, it startled her. Still groggy, she got up to answer it.

"Hi, Abbie," she heard Ben say. "Listen, I'm sorry about today. You may have been ordering me around, but I shouldn't have been so mean to you. I don't know what else to say. Will you forgive me?"

Abbie took a moment to answer. Her eyes were still burning from the tears. She did love Ben, but she was still angry.

"I don't know," she finally said. "You were pretty unreasonable. And we came pretty close to getting caught fighting in the office today."

"Look, I made a mistake," Ben said wearily. "Can't we just forget it?"

Abbie was determined not to back down. "I'm not ready to forget it yet," she said. "I need some time to think things over."

When she hung up the phone, Abbie started to cry all over again.

Tuesday morning Abbie awoke with the same aching despair she had felt the first time she and Ben fought. Oliver was curled up on the bed next to her, purring in his sleep.

"What do *you* know?" she asked him. Oliver continued sleeping. "You're only a cat. You've never had a problem in your life."

In the office, Abbie and Ben went out of their way to be pleasant to each other. But as the week progressed, Abbie became more and more depressed. She began to think that even fighting would be better than this forced politeness.

By Friday, Abbie was so lonely and miserable she almost asked Ben if he wanted to make up. She was still considering it when the telephone rang.

"Dr. Howell's office. This is Abbie," she said.

"Hello, Abbie," said a deep male voice. "This is Ed Haggerty. Do you remember me? I was one of Dr. Stein's patients."

"Yes, I do," said Abbie, surprised by the call. As she remembered, Ed was friendly and very good-looking.

"I hope you don't mind that I got your number from Dr. Stein," Ed continued. "I was wondering if you'd like to get together some time."

Abbie glanced over her shoulder to make sure Ben was in the examining room with Dr. Howell. She didn't know what to say. She hadn't really thought about dating anyone new. But she was so lonely, and at this point she and Ben weren't really seeing each other anymore. "What do I have to lose?" she thought.

"Sure," Abbie said to Ed, "that would be great."

"Are you busy tomorrow evening?" Ed asked.

"No, tomorrow would be fine," Abbie replied. She wanted to get off the phone before Ben came out of the examining room. "What time?"

"How about seven?" he suggested.

"OK," said Abbie. "I live at 233 Pinecrest Street, Apartment 4. See you at seven." Abbie put the receiver down quickly.

Saturday night, Abbie held Oliver on her lap as she sat waiting for Ed to pick her up. She felt nervous. It had been more than two months since she had gone out with anyone except Ben. What would she talk about?

As it turned out, Abbie didn't have to talk much to Ed for a while. He took her to see the latest Harrison Ford movie. They didn't really get a chance to talk until afterward when they stopped at a coffee shop for a snack.

Ed began their conversation by asking Abbie a lot of questions about her job. Then Abbie asked, "What do you do for a living, Ed?"

"I sell life insurance," Ed answered. "I like it because I get to travel, and I enjoy meeting a lot of different people."

"That sounds like a good job," Abbie remarked, trying to sound interested. Ed was nice, and he probably *was* interesting. But Abbie's mind was on Ben and how much fun she always had with him.

Still, she was determined to give Ed a chance. If Ben were going to continue being unreasonable, she wanted *someone* to go out with. On the way home, Ed asked her out again for the following Saturday. Abbie agreed.

"I'll be away on business this week," Ed told her, "so I won't be able to call you before Saturday. Shall I pick you up at seven again?"

"That'd be fine. See you next week," Abbie answered.

They reached Abbie's building. Ed gave Abbie a quick kiss, and they thanked each other for the evening. Then Ed left.

Monday morning Abbie couldn't wait to see Ben. She had missed him more than ever over the weekend. Now she longed just to see his smile and hear his voice. When she arrived at work at the usual time, Ben wasn't there. A message on the answering machine said that Dr. Howell would be late.

Looking at the appointment book, Abbie saw trouble ahead that morning. The first two appointments were for Gabriel, the Siamese cat, and his archenemy, the German shepherd named Melissa. "Why did I schedule those two together?" she wondered. She wished Ben would hurry up. He still wasn't there when Gabriel and Melissa arrived at the same time.

"The doctor will be a little late," Abbie said to the owners. She noticed that Melissa, as usual, was not on a leash.

As soon as the owners sat down, Gabriel started his hissing and spitting act. But apparently Melissa wasn't going to take it. In two giant bounds, she crossed the waiting room. Gabriel took a flying leap and landed on Melissa's back. Melissa shook him off, and Gabriel got even by raking his claws across Melissa's nose. But he got too close to the huge German shepherd's mouth. Melissa's jaws clamped down on the back of Gabriel's neck. Melissa's owner screamed. Abbie stepped forward to help but was afraid Gabriel would be hurt if she pulled him away from Melissa. When Ben came bursting through the doorway a second later, Melissa was shaking Gabriel back and forth by the scruff of his neck.

Abbie and Ben looked at each other in panic. Then Ben yelled, "Water! Melissa hates water!" They ran into the back room and came back, Ben carrying a coffee pot and Abbie with two glasses of cold water.

"Now!" Ben shouted. They emptied their containers of water over the two animals. Melissa instantly dropped Gabriel and ran shivering and whimpering back to her owner. Gabriel shook himself furiously, trying to shake the water out of his fur.

Neither animal was hurt seriously. By the time Dr. Howell arrived, the water was cleaned up. Both Gabriel and Melissa had been toweled dry. Even the two owners had calmed down a little. Ben explained the situation to the vet.

When the waiting room was empty, Dr. Howell congratulated Ben and Abbie on their quick action.

"You two certainly do make a good team," the doctor said.

"I know," said Ben, giving Abbie his most loving smile.

As soon as Dr. Howell disappeared into his office, Abbie found herself in Ben's arms.

The rest of the week went perfectly. Ben was his old self at work. Abbie was careful not to sound bossy, and Ben grew to appreciate Abbie's efficiency in the office. On Friday evening they double-dated with Suzanne and her fiancé and had a wonderful time.

Saturday was a beautiful day. The leaves were beginning to turn an early-autumn shade of red and yellow, and the sky was a deep bright blue. Abbie and Ben took a long bike ride, stopping by the shore of a lake for a picnic lunch.

Abbie gazed into the still, clear water. Then, her dark hair shining in the sun, she turned to Ben and gave him a long, tender kiss.

"I love you, Abbie," Ben whispered, holding her close. "I'm so glad we're together again."

They were both tired when they got back to Abbie's apartment. Ben relaxed on the couch, forcing Oliver to wake up and move. Abbie snuggled up next to him. They were both asleep when the doorbell woke them up.

"Who could that be?" Abbie wondered sleepily. Then suddenly, to her horror, she realized that she had entirely forgotten about her date with Ed Haggerty. In fact, she had been so happy to be reunited with Ben that she had forgotten Ed even existed.

"My date!" she cried as she jumped up from the couch. Then, halfway to the door, she stopped and clasped her hand over her mouth. "I've made a terrible mistake," she said to Ben. "But just give me a chance to explain and you'll understand. I promise."

Ben looked sleepy and confused. Abbie wished she had more time to think, but the doorbell rang again. "I've done it now," she said angrily to herself as she walked the rest of the way to the door. As she opened it, she was afraid she was saying good-bye to happiness forever.

"Hi, Abbie," Ed began, but he stopped when he saw Ben.

Ben stood up. "Don't mind me," he said sarcastically. "I'm sure Abbie meant to get rid of me before you came, but she fell asleep."

"Ben," Abbie pleaded, "I told you I could explain. You've got to give me a chance." Desperately, she grabbed his arm. "Please don't go." But Ben pulled away from her, slamming the door as he left.

"I'm really sorry about this," Abbie managed to say to Ed through her sobs. "It's all my fault." She explained to Ed what had happened, hoping his feelings wouldn't be too hurt.

"It's OK, Abbie," he said understandingly. "I know you didn't mean any harm. I'll bet if you give Ben a chance to cool off, he'll come around. Good luck." He patted Abbie on the shoulder as he walked out the door.

Frantically, Abbie dialed Ben's number, even though she knew he wouldn't be home yet. Of course, there was no answer. When he didn't answer late that night or all day Sunday, Abbie realized that Ben was purposely not answering.

At work on Monday morning, Abbie felt both miserable and angry. She couldn't even look at Ben for fear she would either scream or cry.

At lunchtime, Ben approached Abbie's desk as if she were Gabriel the cat about to spring at him any second. "Could we talk?" he asked, afraid to look her in the eye.

"If you wanted to talk, why didn't you answer your phone?" she snapped.

"I needed to cool down first," he said quietly. Ben seemed sincerely sorry, but

Abbie's hurt and anger kept her from responding sympathetically.

"Well, it took you just a little too long," she said bitterly. "I'm afraid it's too late."

Before Ben could reply, Mrs. Kelly and her six-year-old daughter Kathy came in. Mrs. Kelly was carrying their white cat, Puff. Usually a calm, agreeable animal, Puff was making a terrible howling sound. Mrs. Kelly looked panicky, and Kathy was crying hysterically.

In a second Ben had Puff in his arms. "What happened?" he asked.

"She was hit by a car," Mrs. Kelly said. "I can't tell what's wrong with her, but she keeps making this awful sound. She must be in pain."

"Is she going to die?" Kathy sobbed.

"We're going to take very good care of her," Ben told Kathy, stroking the little girl's hair gently. "The first thing we'll do is give her a little shot so nothing will hurt her. Then we'll do our best to make her better."

Ben took Puff into the examining room. Dr. Howell was just finishing up with Mrs. Velez's poodle.

Ben had been so gentle and reassuring that both Kathy and Mrs. Kelly had calmed down. Abbie took over, following Ben's example.

"Would you like me to read a story to you?" she asked Kathy, picking up a children's book Dr. Howell kept in the waiting room. Kathy nodded shyly.

As she read, Abbie thought about how wonderful and caring Ben could be when he didn't let his temper get out of hand. "I guess I'm not perfect, either," she admitted to herself.

Abbie kept Kathy busy until Ben finally came back into the waiting room.

"Good news," he said. "Puff will need a cast on her back leg for a while, but she'll be fine."

Kathy ran to Ben and threw her arms around him. Abbie had to fight back the tears. She wished she could hug Ben, too.

After Mrs. Kelly and Kathy were gone, Abbie said to Ben, "I'm sorry about the way I acted. Would you still be willing to talk?"

Ben nodded, and then smiled for the first time that day.

After work Ben and Abbie biked to the pond next to the restaurant where they had first said they loved each other. They sat on a bench by the pond and watched the sun set. Abbie tried to explain to Ben why Ed had come to her apartment Saturday.

"I know you feel bad about the mix-up, Abbie," Ben said. "But I still can't understand why you'd even want to go out with someone else."

"Oh, Ben," Abbie sighed. "Every moment I spent with Ed I was thinking of you. I went out with him because I was lonely. And part of me wanted to get back at you for being mean. But I never really *wanted* to go out with anyone else. I don't want anyone but you." She glanced at him with a pleading look in her eyes.

"It's all right, Abbie," Ben reassured her. "I guess I felt lonely, too. Are we still a team?" He looked hopeful.

"Oh, yes," Abbie responded. "I miss you so much when we're apart. I really love you, Ben. Please, let's both try to control our tempers. I can't stand it when we fight."

"That's exactly what I was going to say," said Ben. "Let's kiss and make up. But Abbie, this time, let's make it forever."

Abbie lifted her face to his. As she closed her eyes, she knew Ben's words were true. This would be forever.